The Muscle Ladder Cookbook Inspired By Jeff Nippard's Teachings

Quick and Easy Wholesome Healthy Recipes for Building Muscles, Getting Lean, and Staying Healthy

Michelle C. Huff

Disclaimer

This book is intended for informational and educational purposes only. The content is not meant to be a substitute for professional medical advice, diagnosis, or treatment. Always seek the guidance of your physician or other qualified health provider with any questions you may have regarding a medical condition or dietary plan. The author, Michelle C. Huff, is not responsible for any adverse effects, consequences, or damages resulting from the use or application of the information in this book.

The recipes and nutritional information provided are based on general recommendations and should be adapted to suit individual needs. Results may vary, and it is important to consult with a healthcare professional before making any significant changes to your diet or lifestyle, particularly if you have any pre-existing medical conditions.

Introduction

├───────────────────────────────────┤

The Journey to Building a Stronger Body

Achieving a lean, muscular physique is a shared dream for many, but often the path to that goal is clouded by conflicting advice, misleading trends, and unnecessary complexity. The truth is, building muscle and losing fat doesn't have to feel like navigating a maze. It can be straightforward, efficient, and enjoyable—if you understand the fundamentals.

That's where The Muscle Ladder comes in. This isn't just another fitness book filled with flashy promises and gimmicks. It's a roadmap, rooted in science and real-world results, that will guide you step by step toward transforming your body and, by extension, your life. This cookbook is an extension of that philosophy, designed to simplify one of the most critical yet often misunderstood aspects of fitness: nutrition.

Why Nutrition Matters More Than You Think

You can have the best training program in the world, one that's meticulously designed to push your body to its limits and beyond. But if your nutrition doesn't align with your goals, all that effort in the gym can feel like spinning your wheels in the mud. Nutrition is not just an afterthought; it's the foundation of everything.

Think of your body as a high-performance machine. You wouldn't pour low-quality fuel into a sports car and expect it to perform at its peak. The same applies to your body. Proper nutrition provides the building blocks your muscles need to repair and grow, the energy to power through workouts, and the balance to support recovery and overall health.

The Muscle Ladder Cookbook: Your Nutritional Toolbox

This cookbook is not about restriction or endless plain chicken breasts and broccoli. Instead, it's about flexibility, variety, and flavor. Each recipe has been carefully designed to:

- **Support your fitness goals:** Whether you're focused on gaining muscle, cutting fat, or staying in peak condition, these meals fit seamlessly into your plan.
- **Simplify meal preparation:** With easy-to-follow instructions and minimal prep time, the recipes make it convenient to stay on track.
- **Deliver maximum nutrition:** Every ingredient is chosen with purpose—to provide the right balance of macronutrients and essential vitamins to fuel your progress.

Breaking Down the Essentials

Before diving into the recipes, it's important to understand the principles that tie everything together. These principles are the backbone of The Muscle Ladder, and they'll guide you in making smart decisions about your diet, even beyond this book.

Consistency is King
- Progress comes from what you do consistently, not occasionally. A single healthy meal won't change your body, just as one indulgent treat won't derail your progress. This book is designed to help you stay consistent by making your meals something to look forward to.

Macronutrients Matter
- Every recipe in this book is balanced with the right proportions of protein, carbohydrates, and fats. Understanding your macronutrient needs is critical, as they directly influence your body composition and energy levels.

Timing Enhances Results
- While total daily intake matters most, strategically timed meals can optimize your workouts and recovery. Recipes in this book are categorized to fit specific needs,

whether it's fueling a morning session or repairing muscles after an intense evening lift.

Flexibility Equals Sustainability

- No one wants to eat the same three meals on repeat forever. This cookbook embraces variety to keep things exciting and sustainable. Flexibility is what makes long-term adherence possible, and that's the key to lasting results.

What's Next

This introduction is just the beginning. Think of it as the warm-up before a workout—a chance to prime your mind and set your intentions. From here, we'll delve into the specific building blocks of nutrition, explore the science behind what makes a meal effective, and, of course, dive into a collection of recipes that will help you achieve your goals.

With The Muscle Ladder Cookbook, you're not just preparing meals—you're building a foundation for success. Let's get started!

Chapter 1

The Muscle-Building Fundamentals

When it comes to transforming your physique, most people instinctively focus on their workout routines: how much weight to lift, how many reps to perform, and which exercises are best. But here's the truth: no matter how solid your training program is, if your nutrition is off, you're leaving gains on the table. Nutrition isn't just part of the equation—it's the backbone of your success.

Why Nutrition is Key

Imagine trying to build a house without bricks or cement. That's exactly what training without proper nutrition looks like. Your body requires specific nutrients to repair and grow muscle tissue, restore energy, and maintain optimal performance. Without those building blocks, you'll struggle to see progress, no matter how hard you work in the gym.

Your diet provides the raw materials your body needs to:

1. **Repair and rebuild** muscle fibers damaged during training.
2. **Replenish** the glycogen stores in your muscles to fuel future workouts.
3. **Support overall recovery,** including hormonal and metabolic balance.

But nutrition is more than hitting numbers on a spreadsheet—it's about sustainability and enjoyment. You can only stick to a plan if you enjoy what you're eating. Bland, uninspired meals might work for a week or two, but they'll eventually leave you frustrated and craving variety. That's why the recipes in this book are designed to be flavorful, diverse, and easy to prepare. You'll not only meet your goals but also enjoy the process.

The Importance of Macronutrients

If you've spent any time researching fitness nutrition, you've undoubtedly come across the term "macros." Short for macronutrients, these are the three key nutrients your body needs in large amounts: **protein, carbohydrates, and fats.** Let's break them down:

Protein: The Builder

Protein is the star player in muscle building. It's made up of amino acids, the "building blocks" your body uses to repair and grow muscle tissue after workouts. Without enough protein, you'll find it nearly impossible to build or even maintain muscle.

Aim for high-quality protein sources such as lean meats, eggs, fish, and dairy. Plant-based options like lentils, beans, and tofu are excellent choices for vegetarians. Each recipe in this book is packed with optimal protein content to ensure your muscles are getting what they need.

Carbohydrates: The Fuel

Carbs are your body's primary energy source, especially during intense workouts. They replenish glycogen, which is stored in your muscles and liver to fuel performance. Complex carbs like oats, sweet potatoes, and whole grains are ideal for sustained energy, while simpler carbs, like fruits, can provide a quick boost.

A balance of complex and simple carbs ensures that you're energized for your workouts and recovering effectively afterward. Recipes in this book strategically incorporate carbs to optimize your performance and recovery.

Fats: The Hormonal Regulator

Fats often get a bad rap, but they play a critical role in hormone production and overall health. Healthy fats from sources like avocados, nuts, seeds, and fatty fish support testosterone production—a key hormone for muscle growth—and provide long-lasting energy.

Each recipe balances fat intake to ensure you're reaping the benefits without overdoing it.

Meal Timing: Making Every Bite Count

You've probably heard the phrase, "It's not what you eat; it's when you eat." While that's an oversimplification, timing your meals around your training can enhance your results. Here's why it matters:

Pre-Workout Nutrition

The goal of your pre-workout meal is to provide enough energy for you to perform at your best. A combination of carbs for quick energy and protein for muscle support is ideal.

Recipes like protein-packed smoothies or high-carb breakfast bowls are perfect for fueling up before hitting the gym.

Post-Workout Nutrition

After a workout, your body is like a sponge, ready to absorb nutrients to repair muscle and replenish glycogen. A meal high in protein and fast-digesting carbs is ideal.

This cookbook includes recipes like grilled chicken with sweet potato mash or post-workout recovery shakes to give your body exactly what it needs.

Throughout the Day

While pre- and post-workout meals are crucial, don't neglect the rest of the day. Eating balanced meals at regular intervals ensures your body has a steady supply of nutrients for repair, growth, and energy.

Recipes like midday muscle boosters and high-protein dinner feasts keep you on track without feeling deprived.

What This Means for You

Understanding the role of macronutrients and meal timing might seem overwhelming at first, but it's simpler than it looks. Once you know your targets, it becomes second nature. The recipes in this book take the guesswork out of planning and help you align your nutrition with your fitness goals.

Whether you're fueling up for a big lift, recovering from a grueling session, or simply staying consistent day-to-day, this cookbook has you covered. Nutrition isn't just fuel for your body—it's the secret weapon that makes all the difference in building a stronger, leaner you.

Let's move forward and explore how you can turn these fundamentals into action with meals that are as effective as they are delicious.

Chapter 2

Fueling the Ladder: Recipes for Strength and Recovery

When it comes to achieving your fitness goals, every meal is an opportunity to take a step closer to success. Nutrition isn't just about hitting calorie and macronutrient targets —it's about choosing the right foods at the right times to fuel your workouts, enhance recovery, and maintain peak performance throughout your day.

The recipes in this cookbook are crafted with these goals in mind. They're designed to be simple, flexible, and most importantly, effective. Whether you're gearing up for an intense session, recovering from a grueling workout, or maintaining your momentum through a busy day, there's a meal here to support you.

Breakfast Power Meals

Breakfast is more than just the first meal of the day—it's your launchpad. The right breakfast will kickstart your metabolism, replenish energy stores after a night of fasting, and set the tone for your day.

These recipes are packed with high-quality protein and slow-digesting carbohydrates to fuel your morning workouts or provide sustained energy for your daily tasks. From protein pancakes to overnight oats loaded with berries and nuts, these meals are as energizing as they are delicious.

Start your day strong, and you'll notice the difference in your performance and focus.

Midday Muscle Boosters

Let's face it—midday meals often become an afterthought in the hustle and bustle of life. But skipping or skimping on lunch can leave you feeling sluggish and unfocused, sabotaging your productivity and your workouts.

The recipes in this section are designed to be quick to prepare and easy to eat, without compromising on quality. Think grilled chicken wraps, quinoa bowls loaded with vegetables, and protein-packed salads. These meals provide the perfect balance of macronutrients to keep your energy steady and your muscles fueled.

Pre-Workout Energy Snacks

The meal you eat before your workout can make or break your performance. Too heavy, and you'll feel sluggish; too light, and you'll run out of energy. The key is a snack that's rich in easily digestible carbs for quick energy and a moderate amount of protein for muscle support.

This section includes recipes like banana and peanut butter rice cakes, Greek yogurt parfaits with granola, and fruit smoothies with a protein kick. These snacks are portable, quick to prepare, and will have you feeling strong and ready to dominate your session.

High-Protein Dinner Feasts

Dinner is your chance to end the day on a strong note. It's the meal that will support overnight recovery, providing your body with the nutrients it needs to repair and rebuild while you sleep.

These recipes include baked chicken thighs with roasted vegetables, beef and sweet potato shepherd's pie, and seared tofu with stir-fried broccoli. They're designed to be filling, nutrient-dense, and aligned with your fitness goals, so you can wake up ready to tackle another day

The Bottom Line

Every recipe in this section is more than just a meal—it's a tool for success. They're easy to prepare, adaptable to your schedule, and packed with the nutrients your body needs to thrive. By choosing meals that align with your goals, you'll be fueling not just your workouts, but your overall progress.

With these recipes, you'll never have to wonder, "What should I eat?" Instead, you'll feel confident knowing that every bite is helping you climb higher on The Muscle Ladder. Let's get cooking!

Breakfast Power Meals

Keto Green Smoothie

Serves: 2 | Prep Time: 10 mins

Ingredients

- 2 tablespoons flax seed meal
- 2 cups frozen spinach
- 2 tablespoons chia seeds
- 1 scoop whey protein
- 5 cubes ice + 3 cups water

Directions

- In a blender, combine all the ingredients and process until smooth.
- Transfer into two glasses and serve right away.

Nutrition

- Calories: 116
- Carbs: 6g
- Fats: 4g
- Proteins: 13.6g
- Sodium: 54mg
- Sugar: 0.7g

Bacon and Eggs

Serves: 12 | Prep Time: 15 mins

Ingredients

- ½ teaspoon dried organic thyme
- 24 organic bacon slices
- 7 oz full-fat cream cheese
- 12 hard-cooked organic large eggs, peeled, yolks removed, and sliced lengthwise

Directions

- Grease a baking dish and preheat the oven to 400 degrees F.
- In a small bowl, combine the cream cheese and thyme and set aside.
- Pour the cream cheese mixture into the egg white halves. Next, cover them with the remaining half of egg white.
- Wrap two pieces of bacon tightly around each egg.
- Transfer the covered eggs to the oven after placing them in the baking dish.
- Bake for around half an hour.
- Serve immediately out of the oven.

Nutrition

- Calories: 326
- Carbs: 1.4g
- Fats: 26g
- Proteins: 20.9g
- Sodium: 988mg
- Sugar: 0.4g

Creamy Keto Cinnamon Smoothie

Serves: 1 | Prep Time: 10 mins

Ingredients
- ½ cup water + few ice cubes
- ½ cup coconut milk
- ½ teaspoon cinnamon
- ¼ cup vanilla whey protein
- 1 tablespoon MCT oil
- 1 tablespoon ground chia seeds

Directions
- In a blender, combine all the ingredients and process until smooth.
- Transfer to a glass and serve right away.

Nutrition
- Calories: 406
- Carbs: 11.3g
- Fats: 45.6g
- Proteins: 9.4g
- Sodium: 32mg
- Sugar: 4.3g

Scrambled Eggs with Mushrooms and Cheese

Serves: 4 | Prep Time: 20 mins

Ingredients

- 4 tablespoons butter
- 8 eggs
- 4 tablespoons Parmesan cheese, shredded
- Salt and black pepper, to taste
- 1 cup fresh mushrooms, chopped finely

Directions

- In a bowl, combine eggs, salt, and black pepper; beat thoroughly.
- Add the beaten eggs to a non-stick pan with melted butter.
- Add the mushrooms and Parmesan cheese after cooking for
- approximately five minutes.
- Cook for a further five minutes, stirring now and then.
- Wait approximately three minutes before using your hands to eat the meal because it will be hot after cooking.

Nutrition

- Calories: 203
- Carbs: 1.2g
- Fats: 17.5g
- Proteins: 11.2g
- Sodium: 217mg
- Sugar: 0.8g

Peanut Butter Chocolate Smoothie

Serves: 1 | Prep Time: 5 mins

Ingredients
- 1 tablespoon unsweetened cocoa powder
- 1 cup unsweetened coconut milk
- 1 tablespoon unsweetened peanut butter
- 1 pinch sea salt
- 5 drops stevia

Directions
- In a blender, combine all the ingredients and process until smooth.
- Transfer to a glass and serve right away.

Nutrition

- Calories: 79
- Carbs: 6.4g
- Fats: 5.7g
- Proteins: 3.6g
- Sodium: 235mg
- Sugar: 1.6g

Cream Cheese Pancakes

Serves: 4 | Prep Time: 12 mins

Ingredients
- 2 eggs
- ½ teaspoon cinnamon
- 2 oz cream cheese
- 1 teaspoon granulated sugar substitute
- ½ cup almond flour

Directions
- In a blender, combine all the ingredients and pulse until smooth.
- After transferring the mixture to a medium bowl, set it aside for approximately three minutes.
- Add ¼ of the mixture to a large non-stick skillet that has been greased with butter.
- Cook for approximately two minutes, or until golden brown, tilting the pan to distribute the mixture.
- After flipping the pancakes, fry them for approximately one minute on the other side.
- Top with your preferred berries and repeat in batches with the leftover mixture.

Nutrition
- Calories: 170
- Carbs: 4.3g
- Fats: 14.3g
- Proteins: 6.9g
- Sodium: 81mg
- Sugar: 0.2g

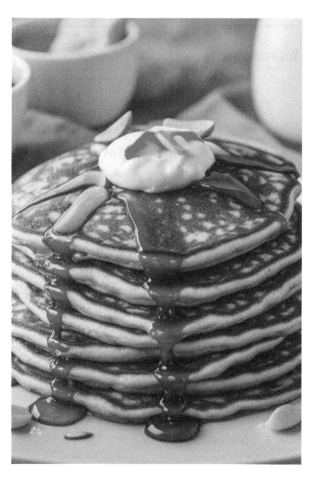

Chocolate Coconut Keto Smoothie

Serves: 1 | Prep Time: 10 mins

Ingredients
- 2 tablespoons unsweetened cocoa powder
- ¾ cup full-fat organic coconut milk
- 10 drops liquid coconut stevia
- 2 scoops collagen protein
- 4 ice cubes

Directions
- In a blender, combine all the ingredients and process until smooth.
- Transfer to a glass and serve right away.

Nutrition
- Calories: 500
- Carbs: 12g
- Fats: 38g
- Proteins: 26g
- Sodium: 120mg
- Sugar: 3g

Coconut Chia Pudding

Serves: 4 | Prep Time: 25 mins

Ingredients
- 1 cup full-fat coconut milk
- ¼ cup chia seeds
- ½ tablespoon honey
- 2 tablespoons almonds
- ¼ cup raspberries

Directions
- In a bowl, combine the honey, chia seeds, and coconut milk; chill overnight.
- To serve, take out of the refrigerator and garnish with almonds and raspberries.

Nutrition
- Calories: 158
- Carbs: 6.5g
- Fats: 14.1g
- Proteins: 2g
- Sodium: 16mg
- Sugar: 3.6g

- Calories: 227
- Carbs: 12.8g
- Fats: 20g
- Proteins: 2.5g
- Sodium: 11mg
- Sugar: 2.3g

Raspberry Avocado Smoothie

Serves: 2 | Prep Time: 10 mins

Ingredients

- 1¼ cups water
- 1 ripe avocado, peeled and pit removed
- 3 tablespoons lemon juice
- ½ cup frozen unsweetened raspberries
- 2 scoops stevia

Directions

- In a blender, combine all the ingredients and process until smooth.
- Serve right away after pouring into two glasses.

Nutrition

Morning Hash

Serves: 2/Prep Time: 30 mins

Ingredients
- ½ teaspoon dried thyme, crushed
- ½ small onion, chopped
- 1 tablespoon butter
- ½ cup cauliflower florets, boiled
- ¼ cup heavy cream
- Salt and black pepper, to taste
- ½ pound cooked turkey meat, chopped

Directions
- In a chopper, cut the cauliflower florets and set aside.
- In a skillet, add the butter and onions, and cook for approximately three minutes.
- Sauté the chopped cauliflower for an additional three minutes or so.
- Cook for about six minutes after adding the turkey.
- Add heavy cream and simmer, stirring frequently, for about 2 minutes.
- Serve it right away or store it in the refrigerator for up to three days to prepare meals. All you need to do is reheat it in the microwave.

Nutrition
- Calories per serving: 309 Carbohydrates: 3.6g
- Protein: 34.3g
- Fat: 17.1g
- Sugar: 1.4g
- Sodium: 134mg

Spanish Scramble

Serves: 2/Prep Time: 20 mins

Ingredients

- 3 tablespoons butter
- 2 tablespoons scallions, sliced thinly
- 4 large organic eggs
- 1 Serrano chili pepper
- ¼ cup heavy cream
- 2 tablespoons cilantro, chopped finely
- 1 small tomato, chopped
- Salt and black pepper, to taste

Directions

- In a medium bowl, mix together cream, eggs, cilantro, salt, and black pepper.
- In a pan over medium heat, add the butter, tomatoes, and Serrano pepper. Sauté for approximately two minutes.
- Stirring constantly, add the egg mixture to the pan and simmer for approximately 4 minutes.
- Serve right away after garnishing with scallions.
- This scramble can be reheated in a microwave oven and kept in the refrigerator for up to two days for dinner preparation.

Nutrition

- Calories per serving: 180
- Carbohydrates: 2g
- Protein: 6.8g
- Fat: 16.5g
- Sugar: 1.1g
- Sodium: 231mg

Cheese Waffles

Serves: 2/Prep Time: 20 mins

Ingredients
- ½ cup Parmesan cheese, shredded
- 2 organic eggs, beaten
- 1 teaspoon onion powder
- 1 cup mozzarella cheese, shredded
- 1 tablespoon chives, minced
- ½ teaspoon ground black pepper
- 1 cup cauliflower
- 1 teaspoon garlic powder

Directions
- In a bowl, combine all the ingredients and set aside.
- Heat a waffle iron after greasing it.
- Fill the waffle iron with half of the mixture, then cook until golden brown.
- To serve, repeat with the other half of the mixture and serve.
- For extended meal preparation, you may keep these waffles in the refrigerator for up to four days. Slide wax paper between each waffle after placing them in a container.

Nutrition
- Calories per serving: 149
- Carbohydrates: 6.1g
- Protein: 13.3g
- Fat: 8.5g
- Sugar: 2.3g
- Sodium: 228mg

Spinach Frittata

Serves: 2/Prep / Time: 45 mins

Ingredients
- 1½ ounce dried bacon
- 2 ounce spinach, fresh
- 1½ ounce shredded cheese
- ½ tablespoon butter
- ¼ cup heavy whipped cream
- 2 eggs
- Salt and black pepper, to taste

Directions
- Grease a baking dish and preheat the oven to 360 degrees Fahrenheit.
- Add bacon to a skillet with hot butter.
- Add the spinach and cook until crispy.
- Stir well and set aside.

- In a basin, whisk together the cream and eggs, then transfer to the baking dish.
- Transfer to the oven after adding the bacon spinach mixture to the baking dish.
- Take it out of the oven to serve after baking it for about half an hour.
- This frittata can be stored in the refrigerator for up to two days for dinner preparation, and it can be reheated in a microwave oven for later use.

Nutrition
- Calories per serving: 592
- Carbohydrates: 3.9g
- Protein: 39.1g
- Fat: 46.7g
- Sugar: 1.1g
- Sodium: 1533mg

Keto Oatmeal

Serves: 2/Prep Time: 20 mins

Ingredients
- 2 tablespoons flaxseeds
- 2 tablespoons sunflower seeds
- 2 cups coconut milk
- 2 tablespoons chia seeds
- 2 pinches of salt

Directions
- In a saucepan, combine all the ingredients and stir to combine.
- After bringing everything to a boil, let it simmer for roughly seven minutes.
- Transfer to a bowl and serve hot.
- You can prepare your oats more quickly by putting all the seeds in a jar and thoroughly mixing them.

Nutrition
- Calories per serving: 337
- Carbohydrates: 7.8g
- Protein: 4.9g
- Fat: 32.6g
- Sugar: 4.1g
- Sodium: 98mg

Cheese Rolls

Serves: 2/Prep Time: 20 mins

Ingredients
- 2 ounce butter, thinly sliced
- 8 ounce cheddar cheese slices

Directions
- Place the cheese slices on a board and spread butter over each one.
- Serve it as a healthy breakfast after rolling it up.
- These cheese rolls can be frozen for meal preparation by covering them with plastic wrap. To repurpose them, reheat them in a microwave.

Nutrition
- Calories per serving: 330
- Carbohydrates: 0.7g
- Protein: 14.2g
- Fat: 30.3g
- Sugar: 0.3g
- Sodium: 434mg

Midday Muscle Boosters

Salmon Stew

Serves: 2/Prep Time: 20 mins

Ingredients
- 1 pound salmon fillet, sliced
- 1 onion, chopped
- Salt, to taste
- 1 tablespoon butter, melted
- 1 cup fish broth
- ½ teaspoon red chili powder

Directions
- Use red chili powder and salt to season the salmon fillets.
- In a skillet, add the butter and onions, and cook for approximately three minutes.
- Cook the fish for approximately two minutes on each side after adding the seasoning.
- Put the fish broth in and cover.
- Cover and cook over medium heat for about 7 minutes.
- Remove from the dish and serve right away.
- To prepare meals, move the stew to a bowl and let it away to cool. The mixture should be divided into two containers.
- Refrigerate for approximately two days with the containers covered. Before serving, reheat in the microwave.

Nutrition
- Calories per serving: 272
- Carbohydrates: 4.4g
- Protein: 32.1g
- Fat: 14.2g
- Sugar: 1.9g
- Sodium: 275mg

Asparagus Salmon Fillets

Serves: 2/Prep Time: 30 mins

Ingredients
- 1 teaspoon olive oil
- 4 asparagus stalks
- 2 salmon fillets
- ¼ cup butter
- ¼ cup champagne
- Salt and freshly ground black pepper, to taste

Directions
- Grease a baking dish and preheat the oven to 355 degrees F.
- In a bowl, combine all the ingredients and stir to combine.
- Fill the baking dish with this mixture, then place it in the oven.
- After around 20 minutes of baking, serve.
- To prepare meals, put the salmon fillets in a plate and set them away to cool.
- After dividing it into two containers, cover them. Before serving, warm in the microwave after a day in the refrigerator.

Nutrition
- Calories per serving: 475
- Carbohydrates: 1.1g
- Protein: 35.2g
- Fat: 36.8g
- Sugar: 0.5g
- Sodium: 242mg

Crispy Baked Chicken

Serves: 2/Prep Time: 40 mins

Ingredients

- 2 chicken breasts, skinless and boneless
- 2 tablespoons butter
- ¼ teaspoon turmeric powder
- Salt and black pepper, to taste
- ¼ cup sour cream

Directions

- Grease a baking dish with butter and preheat the oven to 360 degrees Fahrenheit.
- In a bowl, season the chicken with salt, black pepper, and turmeric powder.
- Place the chicken in the oven after placing it on the baking dish.
- After baking for approximately ten minutes, serve with sour cream on top.
- To prepare meals, move the chicken to a bowl and leave it there to cool.
- After dividing it into two containers, cover them. Before serving, reheat in the microwave after storing in the refrigerator for up to two days.

Nutrition

- Calories per serving: 304
- Carbohydrates: 1.4g
- Protein: 26.1g
- Fat: 21.6g
- Sugar: 0.1g
- Sodium: 137mg

Sour and Sweet Fish

Serves: 2/Prep Time: 25 mins

Ingredients
- 1 tablespoon vinegar
- 2 drops stevia
- 1 pound fish chunks
- ¼ cup butter, melted
- Salt and black pepper, to taste

Directions
- Cook the fish chunks in a skillet with butter for approximately three minutes.
- Stir constantly while cooking for approximately ten minutes after adding the stevia, salt, and black pepper.
- Transfer to a bowl and serve right away.

- To prepare meals, put the fish in a dish and let it cool.
- Refrigerate for up to two days after dividing it into two containers. Before serving, reheat in the microwave.

Nutrition
- Calories per serving: 258
- Carbohydrates: 2.8g
- Protein: 24.5g
- Fat: 16.7g
- Sugar: 2.7g
- Sodium: 649mg

Creamy Chicken

Serves: 2/Prep Time: 25 mins

Ingredients
- ½ small onion, chopped
- ¼ cup sour cream
- Salt and black pepper, to taste
- 1 tablespoon butter
- ¼ cup mushrooms
- ½ pound chicken breasts

Directions
- In a skillet, heat the butter and then add the mushrooms and onions.
- Add the chicken breasts and salt after about five minutes of sautéing.
- Put the lid on and continue cooking for another five minutes or so.
- Cook for about three minutes after adding the sour cream.

- To serve right away, open the lid and pour the contents into a bowl.
- To prepare meals, place the creamy chicken breasts in a dish and leave to cool.
- Split them into two containers and place a lid on each.
- Before serving, warm in the microwave after refrigerating for two to three days.

Nutrition
- Calories per serving: 335
- Carbohydrates: 2.9g
- Protein: 34g
- Fat: 20.2g
- Sugar: 0.8g
- Sodium: 154mg

Paprika Butter Shrimps

Serves: 2/Prep Time: 30 mins

Ingredients

- ¼ tablespoon smoked paprika
- 1/8 cup sour cream
- ½ pound tiger shrimps
- 1/8 cup butter
- Salt and black pepper, to taste

Directions

- Grease a baking dish and preheat the oven to 390 degrees F.
- In a large basin, combine all the ingredients and pour them into the baking dish.
- Put in the oven and let it bake for fifteen minutes or so.
- To prepare meals, put the paprika shrimp in a dish and let them cool.
- Split it into two containers and place a lid on them. Before serving, warm in the microwave after being refrigerated for one to two days.

Nutrition

- Calories per serving: 330
- Carbohydrates: 1.5g
- Protein: 32.6g
- Fat: 21.5g
- Sugar: 0.2g
- Sodium: 458mg

Bacon Wrapped Asparagus

Serves: 2/Prep Time: 30 mins

Ingredients
- 1/3 cup heavy whipping cream
- 2 bacon slices, precooked
- 4 small spears asparagus
- Salt, to taste
- 1 tablespoon butter

Directions
- Grease a baking sheet with butter and preheat the oven to 360 degrees Fahrenheit.
- In the meantime, combine the cream, salt, and asparagus in a basin.
- Arrange the asparagus in the baking dish after wrapping it with bacon strips.
- After placing the baking dish in the oven, bake it for roughly twenty minutes.
- Take it out of the oven and serve it hot.
- To prepare meals, put the asparagus wrapped in bacon in a dish and let it cool. Split it into two containers and place a lid on them.
- Before serving, warm in the microwave after being refrigerated for approximately two days.

Nutrition
- Calories per serving: 204
- Carbohydrates: 1.4g
- Protein: 5.9g
- Fat: 19.3g
- Sugar: 0.5g
- Sodium: 291mg

Spinach Chicken

Serves: 2/Prep Time: 20 mins

Ingredients
- 2 garlic cloves, minced
- 2 tablespoons unsalted butter, divided
- ¼ cup parmesan cheese, shredded
- ¾ pound chicken tenders
- ¼ cup heavy cream
- 10 ounce frozen spinach, chopped
- Salt and black pepper, to taste

Directions
- Add chicken, salt, and black pepper to a large skillet with 1 tablespoon of heated butter.
- After cooking for approximately three minutes on each side, take the chicken out and place it in a bowl.
- Add the spinach, heavy cream, cheese, and garlic to the skillet with the melted butter.
- After about two minutes of cooking, add the chicken.
- Cook over low heat for about 5 minutes, then serve right away.
- To prepare meals, put the chicken in a dish and let it cool.
- After dividing it into two containers, cover them. Before serving, warm in the microwave after being refrigerated for approximately three days.

Nutrition
- Calories per serving: 288
- Carbohydrates: 3.6g
- Protein: 27.7g
- Fat: 18.3g
- Sugar: 0.3g
- Sodium: 192mg

Chicken with Herbed Butter

Serves: 2/Prep Time: 35 mins

Ingredients

- 1/3 cup baby spinach
- 1 tablespoon lemon juice
- ¾ pound chicken breasts
- 1/3 cup butter
- ¼ cup parsley, chopped
- Salt and black pepper, to taste
- 1/3 teaspoon ginger powder
- 1 garlic clove, minced

Directions

- Grease a baking dish and preheat the oven to 450 degrees F.
- In a bowl, combine parsley, ginger powder, butter, lemon juice, garlic, salt, and black pepper.
- After adding the chicken breasts to the sauce, let them marinate for around half an hour.
- After marinating, place the chicken in the baking dish and put it in the oven.
- Bake for about twenty-five minutes, then serve right away.
- To prepare meals, place the chicken in two containers and keep it in the refrigerator for approximately three days.
- Before serving, reheat in the microwave.

Nutrition

- Calories per serving: 568
- Carbohydrates: 1.6g
- Protein: 44.6g
- Fat: 42.1g
- Sugar: 0.3g
- Sodium: 384mg

Lemongrass Prawns

Serves: 2/Prep Time: 25 mins

Ingredients
- ½ red chili pepper, seeded and chopped
- 2 lemongrass stalks
- ½ pound prawns, deveined and peeled
- 6 tablespoons butter
- ¼ teaspoon smoked paprika

Directions
- Grease a baking dish and preheat the oven to 390 degrees F.
- In a bowl, combine the prawns, butter, smoked paprika, and red chili pepper.
- After marinating for approximately two hours, thread the prawns onto the stalks of lemongrass.
- Place the baking dish with the threaded prawns on it and put it in the oven.
- Bake for 15 minutes or so, then serve right away.
- To prepare the meal, put the prawns in a plate and leave them to cool.
- After dividing it into two containers, cover them.
- Store in the fridge for approximately 4 days, then warm in the microwave before serving.

Nutrition
- Calories per serving: 322
- Carbohydrates: 3.8g
- Protein: 34.8g
- Fat: 18g
- Sugar: 0.1g
- Sodium: 478mg

Stuffed Mushrooms

Serves: 2/Prep Time: 45 mins

Ingredients
- 2 ounce bacon, crumbled
- ½ tablespoon butter
- ¼ teaspoon paprika powder
- 2 portobello mushrooms
- 1 ounce cream cheese
- ¾ tablespoon fresh chives, chopped
- Salt and black pepper, to taste

Directions
- Grease a baking dish and preheat the oven to 400 degrees F.
- Add mushrooms to a skillet with hot butter.
- After around 4 minutes of sautéing, set aside.
- In a bowl, combine cream cheese,
- black pepper, paprika powder, chives, and salt.
- Transfer the mushrooms to the baking dish after stuffing them with this mixture.
- Bake for about 20 minutes after placing in the oven.
- These mushrooms go well with scrambled eggs and can be stored in the refrigerator for up to three days for meal preparation.

Nutrition
- Calories per serving: 570
- Carbohydrates: 4.6g
- Protein: 19.9g
- Fat: 52.8g
- Sugar: 0.8g
- Sodium: 1041mg

Honey Glazed Chicken Drumsticks

Serves: 2/Prep Time: 30 mins

Ingredients

- ½ tablespoon fresh thyme, minced
- 1/8 cup Dijon mustard
- ½ tablespoon fresh rosemary, minced
- ½ tablespoon honey
- 2 chicken drumsticks
- 1 tablespoon olive oil
- Salt and black pepper, to taste

Directions

- Grease a baking dish and preheat the oven to 325 degrees F.
- With the exception of the drumsticks, combine all the ingredients in a basin and well mix.
- Coat the drumsticks liberally with the mixture after adding them.
- To marinate overnight, cover and place in the refrigerator.
- After placing the drumsticks in the baking dish, move them to the oven.
- After around 20 minutes of cooking, serve right away by dishing out.
- To prepare meals, place the chicken drumsticks in a plate and leave them to cool.
- After dividing it into two containers, cover them. Before serving, warm in the microwave after storing for approximately three days.

Nutrition

- Calories per serving: 301
- Carbs: 6g
- Fats: 19.7g
- Proteins:
- 4.5g
- Sugar: 4.5g
- Sodium: 316mg

Keto Zucchini Pizza

Serves: 2/Prep Time: 15 mins

Ingredients
- 1/8 cup spaghetti sauce
- ½ zucchini, cut in circular slices
- ½ cup cream cheese
- Pepperoni slices, for topping
- ½ cup mozzarella cheese, shredded

Directions
- Grease a baking dish and preheat the oven to 350 degrees F.
- Spread spaghetti sauce over the zucchini in the baking dish.
- Add mozzarella cheese and pieces of pepperoni on top.
- After placing the baking dish in the oven, bake it for approximately fifteen minutes.
- Take out of the oven and serve right away.
- Meal preparation tip: Avoid scorching the cheese because it will turn bitter.

Nutrition
- Calories per serving: 445
- Carbohydrates: 3.6g
- Protein: 12.8g
- Fat: 42g
- Sugar: 0.3g
- Sodium: 429mg

Omega-3 Salad

Serves: 2/Prep Time: 15 mins

Ingredients

- ½ pound skinless salmon fillet, cut into 4 steaks
- ¼ tablespoon fresh lime juice
- 1 tablespoon olive oil, divided
- 4 tablespoons sour cream
- ¼ zucchini, cut into small cubes
- ¼ teaspoon jalapeño pepper, seeded and chopped finely
- Salt and black pepper, to taste
- ¼ tablespoon fresh dill, chopped

Directions

- Cook the salmon in a skillet with olive oil for approximately five minutes on each side.
- Add salt and black pepper, stir thoroughly, and serve.
- To serve, combine the cooked salmon with the remaining ingredients in a bowl.
- Meal Prep Tip: Keep it in the refrigerator for no more than a day.

Nutrition

- Calories per serving: 291
- Fat: 21.1g
- Carbohydrates: 2.5g
- Protein: 23.1g
- Sugar: 0.6g
- Sodium: 112mg

Crab Cakes

Serves: 2/Prep Time: 30 mins

Ingredients

- ½ pound lump crabmeat, drained
- 2 tablespoons coconut flour
- 1 tablespoon mayonnaise
- ¼ teaspoon green Tabasco sauce
- 3 tablespoons butter
- 1 small organic egg, beaten
- ¾ tablespoon fresh parsley, chopped
- ½ teaspoon yellow mustard
- Salt and black pepper, to taste

Directions

- In a bowl, combine all the ingredients, excluding the butter.
- Form this mixture into patties and set aside.
- Add patties to a pan with heated butter over medium heat.
- After cooking for roughly ten minutes on each side, serve hot from the dish.
- For meal preparation, you can keep the raw patties in the freezer for up to three weeks.
- To prevent stickiness, arrange the patties in a container with parchment paper between them.

Nutrition

- Calories per serving: 153
- Fat: 10.8g
- Carbohydrates: 6.7g
- Protein: 6.4g
- Sugar: 2.4g
- Sodium: 46mg

Pre-Workout Energy Snacks

Keto Gin Cocktail

Serves: 1 | Prep Time: 10 mins

Ingredients
- 4 blueberries
- 2 ounces dry gin
- 1 teaspoon erythritol, powdered
- 1 can club soda
- ½ ounce fresh lime juice

Directions
- Place the mint and blueberries in a cocktail shaker.
- Add the gin, erythritol, lime juice, and ice after giving it a good shake.
- Strain into a cocktail glass after giving it another shake.
- Pour club soda on top and serve cold.

Nutrition
- Calories: 161
- Carbs: 7.3g
- Fats: 0.1g
- Proteins: 0.2g
- Sodium: 76mg
- Sugar: 1.7g

Parmesan and Garlic Keto Crackers

Serves: 4 | Prep Time: 40 mins

Ingredients

- 1 cup Parmesan cheese, finely grated
- 1 cup almond flour, blanched
- ½ teaspoon garlic powder
- 1 large egg, whisked
- 1 tablespoon butter, melted

Directions

- Grease two big baking sheets and preheat the oven to 350 degrees F.
- In a large bowl, thoroughly combine the parmesan cheese, almond flour, garlic powder, and chives.
- In another bowl, whisk together the butter and eggs.
- Combine the wet and dry ingredients and stir until a dough forms.
- Press the dough until it is ¼ inch thick after dividing it in half.
- Using a pastry cutter, cut each dough sheet into 25 uniformly sized crackers.
- Put the crackers in the oven after arranging them on the baking sheets.
- Allow them to remain in the off oven after baking for approximately fifteen minutes.
- Take it out of the oven and serve it.

Nutrition

- Calories: 304
- Carbs: 7.4g
- Fats: 23.5g
- Proteins: 16.8g
- Sodium: 311mg
- Sugar: 0.2g

Low Carb Dried Cranberries

Serves: 4 | Prep Time: 4 hours 15 mins

Ingredients
- 1 cup granular erythritol
- ½ teaspoon pure orange extract
- 2 (12 ounce) bags fresh cranberries, rinsed and dried
- 4 tablespoons avocado oil

Directions
- Grease a large baking sheet and preheat the oven to 200 degrees Fahrenheit.
- Cut the dried cranberries in half and combine them with the other ingredients in a bowl.
- Arrange the berries on the baking sheet after tossing to ensure they are well coated.
- After around four hours of baking, serve by dishing out.

Nutrition
- Calories: 111
- Carbs: 16.3g
- Fats: 1.8g
- Proteins: 0.2g
- Sodium: 1mg
- Sugar: 6.2g

Keto Sausage Balls

Serves: 6 | Prep Time: 30 mins

Ingredients

- 1 cup almond flour, blanched
- 1 pound bulk Italian sausage
- 1¼ cups sharp cheddar cheese, shredded
- 2 teaspoons baking powder
- 1 large egg

Directions

- Grease a baking sheet and preheat the oven to 360 degrees Fahrenheit.
- In a large bowl, combine all the ingredients and stir until thoroughly combined.
- Using this mixture, form equal-sized balls and place them on the baking sheet.
- Place in the oven and bake until golden brown, about 20 minutes.

Nutrition

- Calories: 477
- Carbs: 5.1g
- Fats: 39g
- Proteins: 25.6g
- Sodium: 732mg
- Sugar: 0.2g

Keto Pistachio Truffles

Serves: 5 | Prep Time: 10 mins

Ingredients

- ¼ teaspoon pure vanilla extract
- ¼ cup pistachios, chopped
- 1 cup mascarpone cheese, softened
- 3 tablespoons erythritol

Directions

- In a small bowl, combine erythritol, vanilla, and mascarpone cheese.
- Make little balls out of this mixture after properly mixing it until it is smooth.
- Before serving, place the truffles in the refrigerator for half an hour after rolling them in a dish of chopped pistachios.

Nutrition

- Calories: 103
- Carbs: 11.3g
- Fats: 7.8g
- Proteins: 6.2g
- Sodium: 58mg
- Sugar: 9.4g

Creamy Basil Baked Sausage

Serves: 12 | Prep Time: 45 min

Ingredients

- 8 oz cream cheese
- 3 pounds Italian chicken sausages
- ¼ cup basil pesto
- 8 oz mozzarella cheese
- ¼ cup heavy cream

Directions

- Grease a large casserole dish and preheat the oven to 400 degrees F.
- Transfer the casserole dish containing the sausages to the oven.
- After around 30 minutes of baking, serve
- In a bowl, combine the pesto, heavy cream, and cream cheese.
- Place the pesto mixture and

- mozzarella cheese on top of the sausage.
- To serve, take it out of the oven after another ten minutes of baking.

Nutrition

- Calories: 342
- Carbs: 8.9g
- Fats: 23.3g
- Proteins: 21.6g
- Sodium: 624mg
- Sugar: 0.5g

Low Carb Tortilla Chips

Serves: 4 | Prep Time: 25 mins

Ingredients
- 2 tablespoons olive oil
- 3 tablespoons lime juice
- 1 tablespoon taco seasoning
- 6 tortillas, low carb

Directions
- Grease a cookie sheet and preheat the oven to 350 degrees F.
- Place each tortilla on a cookie sheet after cutting it into little wedges.
- Spray each tortilla wedge with a mixture of lime juice and olive oil.
- After adding the taco spice, put it in the oven.
- Rotate the pan after around 8 minutes of baking.
- After 8 more minutes of baking, remove from the oven to serve.

Nutrition
- Calories: 147
- Carbs: 17.8g
- Fats: 8g
- Proteins: 2.1g
- Sodium: 174mg
- Sugar: 0.7g

Salmon Mousse Cucumber Rolls

Serves: 2 | Prep Time: 30 mins

Ingredients

- 2 cucumbers, thinly sliced lengthwise
- 4 oz smoked salmon
- 1 tablespoon dill, fresh
- 8 oz cream cheese
- ½ lemon

Directions

- In a bowl, combine the salmon, lemon, cream cheese, and dill and mash well.
- To serve, spread this mixture over the cucumber slices and gently roll them up.

Nutrition

- Calories: 515
- Carbs: 16.2g
- Fats: 42.4g
- Proteins: 21.4g
- Sodium: 1479mg
- Sugar: 5.6g

Italian keto plate

Serves: 3 | Prep Time: 10 mins

Ingredients
- 7 oz. prosciutto, sliced
- 1/3 cup olive oil
- Salt and black pepper, to taste
- 7 oz. fresh mozzarella cheese
- 10 green olives

Directions
- Arrange the olives, mozzarella cheese, and prosciutto on a platter.
- To serve, sprinkle with salt and black pepper and drizzle with olive oil.

Nutrition
- Calories: 505
- Carbs: 3.3g
- Fats: 40.2g
- Proteins: 32.5g
- Sodium: 1572mg
- Sugar: 0g

Broccoli Cheese Soup

Serves: 6 | Prep Time: 5 hours 10 mins

Ingredients

- 1 cup heavy whipping cream
- 2 cups chicken broth
- 2 cups broccoli
- Salt, to taste
- 2 cups cheddar cheese

Directions

- Place the cheddar cheese, broccoli, chicken broth, heavy whipping cream and salt in a crock pot.
- Set the crock pot on LOW and cook for about 5 hours.
- Ladle out in a bowl and serve hot.

Nutrition

- Calories: 244
- Carbs: 3.4g
- Fats: 20.4g
- Proteins: 12.3g
- Sodium: 506mg
- Sugar: 1g

Mediterranean Spinach with Cheese

Serves: 6 | Prep Time: 25 mins

Ingredients

- 2 pounds spinach, chopped
- ½ cup black olives, halved and pitted
- Salt and black pepper, to taste
- 4 tablespoons butter
- 1½ cups feta cheese, grated
- 4 teaspoons fresh lemon zest, grated

Directions

- Grease an air fryer basket and preheat the air fryer to 400 degrees Fahrenheit.
- In a pan of boiling water, cook spinach for approximately 4 minutes. Make sure to drain thoroughly.
- In a bowl, combine butter, spinach, black pepper, and salt.
- Pour the spinach mixture into the basket of an air fryer.
- Cook, tossing once halfway through, for about 15 minutes.
- To serve, transfer to a bowl and mix in the cheese, lemon zest, and olives.

Nutrition

- Calories: 215
- Carbs: 8g
- Fats: 17.5g
- Proteins: 9.9g
- Sodium: 690mg
- Sugar: 2.3g

Cheesy Cauliflower

Serves: 6 | Prep Time: 30 mins

Ingredients
- 2 tablespoons mustard
- ½ cup butter, cut into small pieces
- 2 cauliflower heads, chopped
- 1 cup Parmesan cheese, grated
- 2 teaspoons avocado mayonnaise

Directions
- Grease a baking dish and preheat the oven to 400 degrees F.
- In a bowl, combine avocado mayonnaise and mustard.
- Transfer the cauliflower to a baking tray after coating it with the mustard mixture.
- Add butter and Parmesan cheese on top, then bake for about twenty-five minutes.
- Take it out of the oven and serve it hot.

Nutrition
- Calories: 201
- Carbs: 6.2g
- Fats: 18.9g
- Proteins: 4.3g
- Sodium: 192mg
- Sugar: 2.4g

Parmesan Roasted Bamboo Sprouts

Serves: 6 | Prep Time: 25 mins

Ingredients
- 2 cups Parmesan cheese, grated
- 2 pounds bamboo sprouts
- 4 tablespoons butter
- ½ teaspoon paprika
- Salt and black pepper, to taste

Directions
- Grease a baking dish and preheat the oven to 365 degrees Fahrenheit.
- Put the bamboo sprouts aside after marinating them in a mixture of paprika, butter, salt, and black pepper.
- Put the baking dish with the seasoned bamboo sprouts in the oven.
- Bake for 15 minutes or so, then serve.

Nutrition
- Calories: 162
- Carbs: 4.7g
- Fats: 11.7g
- Proteins: 7.5g
- Sodium: 248mg
- Sugar: 1.4g

Mexican Cheesy Veggies

Serves: 4 | Prep Time: 40 mins

Ingredients
- 1 onion, thinly sliced
- 1 tomato, thinly sliced
- 1 zucchini, sliced
- 1 teaspoon mixed dried herbs
- Salt and black pepper, to taste
- 1 teaspoon olive oil
- 1 cup Mexican cheese, grated

Directions
- Grease a baking dish and preheat the oven to 370 degrees Fahrenheit.
- Drizzle the baking dish with olive oil after layering the vegetables.
- Evenly cover with cheese, then season with salt, black pepper, and herbs.
- Bake for approximately half an hour, then serve hot.

Nutrition
- Calories: 305
- Carbs: 8.3g
- Fats: 22.3g
- Proteins: 15.2g
- Sodium: 370mg
- Sugar: 4.2g

Green Beans with Mushrooms and Bacons

Serves: 4 | Prep Time: 25 mins

Ingredients

- 4 tablespoons onion, minced
- 4 tablespoons butter
- 1 teaspoon garlic, minced
- 4 cooked bacon slices, crumbled
- 2 cups frozen green beans
- 2 (8-ounce) package white mushrooms, sliced
- ¼ teaspoon salt

Directions

- Choose "Sauté" after adding the butter, onions, and garlic to the Instant Pot.
- Add the bacon and salt after about two minutes of sautéing.
- For approximately ten minutes, cook at "High" and "Manual" pressure with the lid closed.
- After choosing "Cancel," carefully perform a natural release.
- Take off the top and mix in the mushrooms and beans.
- After locking the lid once more, cook for approximately seven minutes on both "High" and "Manual" pressure.
- Serve hot after transferring to a bowl.

Nutrition

- Calories: 220
- Carbs: 11.6g
- Fats: 17g
- Proteins: 10g
- Sodium: 488mg
- Sugar: 3.2g

High-Protein Dinner Feasts

Lobster Salad

Serves: 2/Prep Time: 15 mins

Ingredients
- ¼ yellow onion, chopped
- ¼ yellow bell pepper, seeded and chopped
- ¾ pound cooked lobster meat, shredded
- 1 celery stalk, chopped
- Black pepper, to taste
- ¼ cup avocado mayonnaise

Directions
- In a bowl, add all the ingredients and stir until thoroughly blended.
- Serve cold after about three hours in the refrigerator.
- To prepare meals, put the salad in a container and keep it in the refrigerator for approximately two days.

Nutrition
- Calories per serving: 336
- Carbohydrates: 2g
- Protein: 27.2g
- Fat: 25.2g
- Sugar: 1.2g
- Sodium: 926mg

Beef Sausage Pancakes

Serves: 2/Prep Time: 30 mins

Ingredients
- 4 gluten-free Italian beef sausages, sliced
- 1 tablespoon olive oil
- 1/3 large red bell peppers, seeded and sliced thinly
- 1/3 cup spinach
- ¾ teaspoon garlic powder
- 1/3 large green bell peppers, seeded and sliced thinly
- ¾ cup heavy whipped cream
- Salt and black pepper, to taste

Directions
- In a bowl, combine all the ingredients except the whipped cream and set aside.
- In a skillet, add half of the mixture and butter. Cook for approximately 6 minutes on each side
- Repeat with the rest of the mixture, then serve.
- In a separate bowl, beat the whipped cream until it's smooth.
- Serve whipped cream beside the beef sausage pancakes.
- The sausages must be carefully sliced before being combined with other components for meal preparation.

Nutrition
- Calories per serving: 415
- Carbohydrates: 7g
- Protein: 29.5g
- Fat: 31.6g
- Sugar: 4.3g
- Sodium: 1040mg

Holiday Chicken Salad

Serves: 2/Prep Time: 25 mins

Ingredients

- 1 celery stalk, chopped
- 1½ cups cooked grass-fed chicken, chopped
- ¼ cup fresh cranberries
- ¼ cup sour cream
- ½ apple, chopped
- ¼ yellow onion, chopped
- 1/8 cup almonds, toasted and chopped
- 2-ounce feta cheese, crumbled
- ¼ cup avocado mayonnaise
- Salt and black pepper, to taste

Directions

- In a bowl, combine all the ingredients, excluding the cheese and almonds.
- To serve, sprinkle cheese and nuts over top.
- Meal Prep Tip: If you wish to store the salad, avoid adding cheese and almonds. To serve, cover with plastic wrap and place in the refrigerator.

Nutrition

- Calories per serving: 336
- Carbohydrates: 8.8g
- Protein: 24.5g
- Fat: 23.2g
- Sugar: 5.4g
- Sodium: 383mg

Luncheon Fancy Salad

Serves: 2/Prep Time: 40 mins

Ingredients
- 6-ounce cooked salmon, chopped
- 1 tablespoon fresh dill, chopped
- Salt and black pepper, to taste
- 4 hard-boiled grass-fed eggs, peeled and cubed
- 2 celery stalks, chopped
- ½ yellow onion, chopped
- ¾ cup avocado mayonnaise

Directions
- In a bowl, combine all the ingredients and stir until thoroughly blended.
- To serve, cover with plastic wrap and place in the refrigerator for approximately three hours.
- To prepare meals, store the salad in the refrigerator for up to three days.

Nutrition
- Calories per serving: 303
- Carbohydrates: 1.7g
- Protein: 10.3g
- Fat: 30g
- Sugar: 1g
- Sodium: 314mg

Italian Platter

Serves: 2/Prep Time: 45 mins

Ingredients
- 1 garlic clove, minced
- 5-ounce fresh button mushrooms, sliced
- 1/8 cup unsalted butter
- ¼ teaspoon dried thyme
- 1/3 cup heavy whipping cream
- Salt and black pepper, to taste
- 2 (6-ounce) grass-fed New York strip steaks

Directions
- Grease the grill and preheat it to medium heat.
- After adding salt and black pepper to the steaks, place them on the grill.
- After grilling the steaks for approximately ten minutes on each side, serve them on a tray.
- In a pan, combine butter, mushrooms, salt, and black pepper. Cook for approximately ten minutes.
- Sauté the garlic and thyme together for approximately one minute.
- After adding the cream, simmer for approximately five minutes.
- Serve the steaks hot right away after adding mushroom sauce on top.
- Meal Prep Tip: The mushroom sauce keeps well in the fridge for up to two days. Avoid using too much or too little salt and black pepper when seasoning the steaks.

Nutrition
- Calories per serving: 332
- Carbohydrates: 3.2g
- Protein: 41.8g
- Fat: 20.5g
- Sugar: 1.3g
- Sodium: 181mg

Meat Loaf

Serves: 12/Prep Time: 1 hour 15 mins

Ingredients
- 1 garlic clove, minced
- ½ teaspoon dried thyme, crushed
- ½ pound grass-fed lean ground beef
- 1 organic egg, beaten
- Salt and black pepper, to taste
- ¼ cup onions, chopped
- 1/8 cup sugar-free ketchup
- 2 cups mozzarella cheese, freshly grated
- ¼ cup green bell pepper, seeded and chopped
- ½ cup cheddar cheese, grated
- 1 cup fresh spinach, chopped

Directions
- Grease a baking dish and preheat the oven to 350 degrees F.
- Place everything in a bowl, excluding the cheese and spinach, and stir to combine.
- Place the meat on wax paper, then add the cheese and spinach on top.
- To make a meatloaf, roll the paper around the ingredients.
- Transfer the beef loaf to the baking dish after removing the wax paper.
- Bake it for approximately one hour after placing it in the oven.
- Serve hot from the dish.
- Meal Prep Tip: Before serving, allow the beef loafs to cool for approximately ten minutes to reach room temperature.

Nutrition
- Calories per serving: 439
- Carbohydrates: 8g
- Protein: 40.8g
- Fat: 26g
- Sugar: 1.6g
- Sodium: 587mg

Grilled Steak

Serves: 2/Prep Time: 15 mins

Ingredients
- ¼ cup unsalted butter
- 2 garlic cloves, minced
- ¾ pound beef top sirloin steaks
- ¾ teaspoon dried rosemary, crushed
- 2 oz. parmesan cheese, shredded
- Salt and black pepper, to taste

Directions
- Grease and preheat the grill.
- Use salt and black pepper to season the sirloin steaks.
- After moving the steaks to the grill, cook them for approximately five minutes on each side.
- The steaks should be plated and set aside.

- In the meantime, melt the butter and garlic in a pan.
- Serve the steaks hot after pouring it over them.
- To prepare meals, divide the steaks into two containers and place them in the refrigerator for approximately three days. Prior to serving, reheat in the microwave.

Nutrition
- Calories per serving: 383
- Carbohydrates: 1.5g
- Protein:
- 41.4g
- Fat: 23.6g
- Sugar: 0g
- Sodium: 352mg

Cheese Casserole

Serves: 2/Prep Time: 46 mins

Ingredients
- 2½ ounce marinara sauce
- ½ tablespoon olive oil
- 4 ounce parmesan cheese, shredded
- ½ pound sausages, scrambled
- 4 ounce mozzarella cheese, shredded

Directions
- Grease a baking dish with olive oil and preheat the oven to 375 degrees F.
- Top with half of the marinara sauce, mozzarella, and parmesan cheese after adding half of the sausage scramble.
- After putting the leftover sausage scramble in the baking dish, cover it once more with mozzarella, parmesan, and marinara sauce.
- After transferring, bake for approximately 20 minutes.
- To prepare meals, put the casserole in a dish and let it cool.
- Refrigerate for one to two days after dividing it among six containers. Warm up again in the microwave prior to serving.

Nutrition
- Calories per serving: 353
- Carbohydrates: 5.5g
- Protein: 28.4g
- Fat: 24.3g
- Sugar: 5g
- Sodium: 902mg

Air Fried Simple Steak

Serves: 2/Prep Time: 15 mins

Ingredients
- ½ pound quality cut steaks
- Salt and black pepper, to taste

Directions
- Turn the air fryer on to 385 degrees Fahrenheit.
- Evenly season the steaks with salt and black pepper.
- Put the steak in the basket of an air fryer and cook it for fifteen minutes or so.
- Remove from the dish and serve right away.
- To prepare meals, divide the steaks into two containers and place them in the refrigerator for approximately three days. Before serving, reheat in the microwave.

Nutrition
- Calories per serving: 301
- Carbs: 0g Fats: 25.1g
- Proteins: 19.1g
- Sugar: 0g
- Sodium: 65mg

Rib Eye Steak

Serves: 2/Prep Time: 35 mins

Ingredients
- 1 tablespoon steak rub
- ¾ pound rib eye steak
- 1 tablespoon olive oil

Directions
- Grease a baking tray and preheat the oven to 400 degrees.
- Coat the meat liberally with steak rub after drizzling it with olive oil.
- Transfer the steak from the baking tray to the oven.
- Bake for about twenty-five minutes, then serve right away.
- To prepare meals, place the rib eye steak in a container and keep it in the refrigerator for approximately three days. Before serving, reheat in the microwave.

Nutrition
- Calories per serving: 462
- Carbs: 1g
- Fats: 38.1g
- Proteins: 26.8g
- Sugar: 0g
- Sodium: 307mg

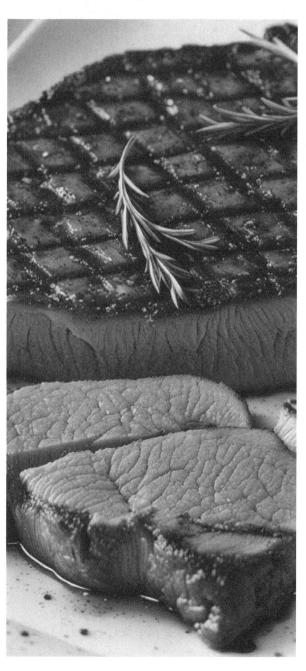

Spicy Skirt Steak

Serves: 2/Prep Time: 40 mins

Ingredients

- 2 tablespoons fresh mint leaves, finely chopped
- 2 tablespoons fresh oregano, finely chopped
- ¾ tablespoon ground cumin
- ¾ cup olive oil
- ¾ teaspoon cayenne pepper
- 2 (8-ounce) skirt steaks
- ¾ cup fresh parsley leaves, finely chopped
- 2 garlic cloves, minced
- 1½ teaspoons smoked paprika
- ¾ teaspoon red pepper flakes, crushed
- 2 tablespoons red wine vinegar
- Salt and black pepper, to taste

Directions

- Grease a baking tray and preheat the oven to 390 degrees F.
- Place everything in a bowl, excluding the steaks, and give it a good toss.
- Add the steaks and thoroughly marinate them.
- Place marinated steaks in a resealable bag with ¼ cup of the herb mixture, and shake to coat thoroughly.
- Set aside the remaining herb combination and refrigerate for approximately one day.
- After taking the steaks out of the fridge, let them sit at room temperature for approximately 30 minutes.
- Transfer the steaks to the oven after arranging them on the baking dish.
- To serve, sprinkle the remaining herb mixture on top after baking for about 25 minutes.
- To prepare meals, place the steaks in a container and keep them in the refrigerator for approximately three days. Before serving, reheat in the microwave.

Nutrition

- Calories per serving: 445
- Carbs: 5.8g
- Fats: 43.1g
- Proteins: 12.9g
- Sugar: 0.5g
- Sodium: 46mg

Leg of Lamb

Serves: 2/Prep Time: 1 hour 30 mins

Ingredients
- ¾ pound leg of lamb
- ¾ tablespoon olive oil
- Salt and black pepper, to taste
- 1 fresh rosemary sprig
- 1 fresh thyme sprig

Directions
- Grease a baking tray and preheat the oven to 330 degrees F.
- After adding salt and black pepper for seasoning, pour olive oil over the leg of lamb.
- Place sprigs of thyme and rosemary over the leg of lamb.
- Transfer the leg of lamb to the oven after placing it on the baking tray.
- After baking for around one and a half hours, serve by dishing out.
- To prepare meals, place the leg of lamb in a container and keep it in the refrigerator for approximately three days. Prior to serving, reheat in the microwave.

Nutrition
- Calories per serving: 325
- Carbs: 0.7g
- Fats: 15.9g
- Proteins: 42.5g
- Sugar: 0g
- Sodium: 115mg

Jamaican Jerk Pork

Serves: 2/Prep Time: 35 mins

Ingredients
- ¾ pound pork shoulder
- ¼ cup whipped cream
- ¼ cup butter, melted
- ¼ cup Jamaican jerk spice blend
- ¼ cup beef broth

Directions
- Put the meat aside after marinating it in a Jamaican jerk spice blend.
- Add marinated pork, butter, and cream to an instant pot.
- After about five minutes of sautéing, add the beef broth.
- For approximately 20 minutes, cook on High Pressure with the cover on.
- Let the pressure drop naturally, then serve.
- To prepare meals, put the pork in a dish and let it away to cool. Refrigerate for approximately three days after dividing it into two containers.
- Prior to serving, reheat in the microwave.

Nutrition
- Calories per serving: 457
- Carbohydrates: 0.3g
- Protein: 27g
- Fat: 38.2g
- Sugar: 0.1g
- Sodium: 209mg

Creamy Turkey Breasts

Serves: 2/Prep Time: 1 hour

Ingredients
- ¼ cup sour cream
- ¼ cup butter
- Salt and black pepper, to taste
- ¾ pound turkey breasts
- ½ cup heavy whipping cream
- 2 garlic cloves, minced

Directions
- Heat the oven to 390 degrees Fahrenheit and apply a little butter to the baking dish.
- In a bowl, combine the butter, garlic, salt, and black pepper to marinate the turkey breasts.
- Top the marinated turkey breasts with sour cream and heavy whipping cream after placing them on a baking tray.
- After about 45 minutes of baking, transfer to a tray.
- To prepare meals, put the tender turkey breasts on a platter and set away to cool.
- Refrigerate for approximately two days after dividing it into two containers.
- Before serving, reheat in the microwave.

Nutrition
- Calories per serving: 304
- Carbohydrates: 4.8g
- Protein: 20.3g
- Fat: 23.1g
- Sugar: 4.1g
- Sodium: 1246mg

Buttered Scallops

Serves: 2/Prep Time: 15 mins

Ingredients

- ¾ pound sea scallops Salt and black pepper, to taste
- 1 tablespoon butter, melted
- ½ tablespoon fresh thyme, minced

Directions

- Grease a baking dish and preheat the oven to 390 degrees F.
- In a large bowl, combine all the ingredients and toss to coat thoroughly.
- Transfer the scallops from the baking dish to the oven.
- After about five minutes of baking, serve by dishing out.
- To prepare meals, you may keep the buttered scallops in the fridge for up to two days in a container. Before serving, you can reheat it in the microwave.

Nutrition

- Calories per serving: 202
- Carbs: 4.4g
- Fats: 7.1g
- Proteins: 28.7g
- Sugar: 0g
- Sodium: 315mg

Week 1 Shopping List

- Salmon fillets (1 lb)
- Eggs (dozen)
- Chicken breasts (4)
- Turkey meat (½ lb)
- Bacon slices (24)
- Full-fat cream cheese (8 oz)
- Parmesan cheese (1 cup shredded)
- Mozzarella cheese (1 cup shredded)
- Butter (1 lb)
- Coconut milk (1 can)
- Flaxseed meal (2 tbsp)
- Chia seeds (¼ cup)
- Almond flour (1 cup)
- Fresh spinach (1 bunch)
- Frozen spinach (2 cups)
- Cauliflower florets (½ cup)
- Mushrooms (1 cup)
- Small onion (2)
- Garlic cloves (4)
- Scallions (1 bunch)
- Heavy cream (1 pint)
- Whey protein powder (1 scoop)
- Unsweetened cocoa powder (1 tbsp)
- Coconut oil (for cooking)
- Sea salt and black pepper
- Cinnamon (1 tsp)
- Raspberries (¼ cup, fresh or frozen)
- Lemon juice (3 tbsp)
- Avocado (1 large, ripe)
- Thyme (½ tsp dried)
- Stevia (liquid or powder)
- Olive oil (for cooking)

Week 1 Meal Plan

Days	Breakfast	Lunch	Snack	Dinner
Day 1	Keto Green Smoothie	Salmon Stew	Parmesan and Garlic Keto Crackers	Creamy Chicken
Day 2	Creamy Keto Cinnamon Smoothie	Bacon and Eggs	Coconut Chia Pudding	Asparagus Salmon Fillets
Day 3	Scrambled Eggs with Mushrooms and Cheese	Morning Hash	Peanut Butter Chocolate Smoothie	Crispy Baked Chicken
Day 4	Cream Cheese Pancakes	Sour and Sweet Fish	Low Carb Tortilla Chips	Paprika Butter Shrimps
Day 5	Chocolate Coconut Keto Smoothie	Spinach Frittata	Keto Sausage Balls	Bacon-Wrapped Asparagus
Day 6	Raspberry Avocado Smoothie	Omega-3 Salad	Parmesan and Garlic Keto Crackers	Chicken with Herbed Butter
Day 7	Keto Oatmeal	Creamy Chicken	Low Carb Dried Cranberries	Spinach Chicken

Week 2 Shopping List

- Grass-fed beef (1 lb)
- Chicken drumsticks (4)
- Italian sausage (1 lb)
- Pork shoulder (½ lb)
- Tiger shrimp (½ lb)
- Smoked salmon (4 oz)
- Cream cheese (8 oz)
- Mozzarella cheese (1 cup shredded)
- Parmesan cheese (½ cup shredded)
- Almond flour (1 cup)
- Coconut flour (2 tbsp)
- Coconut milk (1 can)
- Butter (1 lb)
- Heavy whipping cream (1 pint)
- Fresh spinach (1 bunch)
- Cauliflower (1 head)
- Zucchini (2)
- Asparagus (8 stalks)
- Fresh dill (1 bunch)
- Lemon (1)
- Lime juice (2 tbsp)
- Garlic (5 cloves)
- Green onions/scallions (1 bunch)
- Fresh thyme (½ tsp dried)
- Black olives (¼ cup)
- Fresh parsley (1 bunch)
- Erythritol (½ cup)
- Club soda (1 can)
- Eggs (dozen)
- Olive oil (for cooking)
- Salt and black pepper

Week 2 Meal Plan

Days	Breakfast	Lunch	Snack	Dinner
Day 1	Creamy Basil Baked Sausage	Asparagus Salmon Fillets	Low Carb Tortilla Chips	Crispy Baked Chicken
Day 2	Cheese Rolls	Sour and Sweet Fish	Keto Pistachio Truffles	Bacon Wrapped Asparagus
Day 3	Scrambled Eggs with Mushrooms and Cheese	Omega-3 Salad	Low Carb Dried Cranberries	Paprika Butter Shrimps
Day 4	Chocolate Coconut Keto Smoothie	Crab Cakes	Keto Sausage Balls	Chicken with Herbed Butter
Day 5	Raspberry Avocado Smoothie	Spinach Frittata	Parmesan and Garlic Keto Crackers	Sour and Sweet Fish
Day 6	Keto Oatmeal	Creamy Chicken	Coconut Chia Pudding	Bacon-Wrapped Asparagus
Day 7	Peanut Butter Chocolate Smoothie	Spinach Frittata	Parmesan and Garlic Keto Crackers	Chicken with Herbed Butter

Week 3 Shopping List

- Rib eye steak (1 lb)
- Chicken breasts (4)
- Large shrimp (½ lb)
- Ground beef (½ lb)
- Lump crabmeat (½ lb)
- Prosciutto (7 oz)
- Mozzarella cheese (1 cup shredded)
- Cheddar cheese (1 cup shredded)
- Cream cheese (8 oz)
- Parmesan cheese (½ cup shredded)
- Coconut flour (2 tbsp)
- Almond flour (1 cup)
- Butter (1 lb)
- Heavy cream (1 pint)
- Fresh spinach (1 bunch)
- Zucchini (2)
- Cauliflower (1 head)
- Broccoli (1 bunch)
- Tomato (2)
- Avocado (1 large)
- Fresh basil (1 bunch)
- Fresh mint (1 bunch)
- Fresh parsley (1 bunch)
- Lime juice (2 tbsp)
- Green onions/scallions (1 bunch)
- Garlic (5 cloves)
- Black olives (¼ cup)
- Erythritol (½ cup)
- Eggs (dozen)
- Olive oil (for cooking)
- Salt and black pepper

Week 3 Meal Plan

Days	Breakfast	Lunch	Snack	Dinner
Day 1	Cream Cheese Pancakes	Crab Cakes	Keto Pistachio Truffles	Grilled Rib Eye Steak
Day 2	Chocolate Coconut Keto Smoothie	Spinach Frittata	Parmesan and Garlic Keto Crackers	Creamy Chicken
Day 3	Keto Green Smoothie	Sour and Sweet Fish	Keto Sausage Balls	Paprika Butter Shrimp
Day 4	Peanut Butter Chocolate Smoothie	Mediterranean Spinach with Cheese	Low Carb Tortilla Chips	Bacon-Wrapped Asparagus
Day 5	Scrambled Eggs with Mushrooms and Cheese	Omega-3 Salad	Coconut Chia Pudding	Chicken with Herbed Butter
Day 6	Raspberry Avocado Smoothie	Prosciutto, Mozzarella, and Olive Plate	Parmesan and Garlic Keto Crackers	Crispy Baked Chicken
Day 7	Keto Oatmeal	Spinach Frittata	Low Carb Dried Cranberries	Sour and Sweet Fish

Week 4 Shopping List

- Beef top sirloin steaks (1 lb)
- Chicken thighs (4)
- Grass-fed ground beef (1 lb)
- Sea scallops (½ lb)
- Salmon fillets (½ lb)
- Fresh mozzarella cheese (½ cup)
- Cheddar cheese (1 cup shredded)
- Cream cheese (8 oz)
- Parmesan cheese (½ cup shredded)
- Eggs (dozen)
- Heavy cream (1 pint)
- Full-fat coconut milk (1 can)
- Butter (1 lb)
- Cauliflower (1 head)
- Zucchini (1 large)
- Bell peppers (1 red, 1 green)
- Fresh spinach (1 bunch)
- Fresh basil (1 bunch)
- Fresh rosemary (1 sprig)
- Fresh thyme (1 sprig)
- Black olives (¼ cup)
- Avocado (1 large)
- Lime (1)
- Green onions/scallions (1 bunch)
- Garlic cloves (4)
- Erythritol (½ cup)
- Olive oil (for cooking)
- Salt and black pepper

Week 4 Meal Plan

Days	Breakfast	Lunch	Snack	Dinner
Day 1	Keto Green Smoothie	Stuffed Mushrooms	Parmesan and Garlic Keto Crackers	Beef Sirloin Steak with Herb Butter
Day 2	Creamy Keto Cinnamon Smoothie	Bacon and Eggs	Coconut Chia Pudding	Scallops with Butter and Fresh Thyme
Day 3	Scrambled Eggs with Mushrooms and Cheese	Salmon Fillet with Lemon and Dill	Keto Pistachio Truffles	Creamy Turkey Breasts
Day 4	Raspberry Avocado Smoothie	Prosciutto, Mozzarella, and Olive Plate	Low Carb Tortilla Chips	Crispy Baked Chicken
Day 5	Keto Oatmeal	Meat Loaf	Coconut Chia Pudding	Italian Platter with Fresh Mozzarella and Basil
Day 6	Cream Cheese Pancakes	Omega-3 Salad	Parmesan and Garlic Keto Crackers	Stuffed Portobello Mushrooms
Day 7	Chocolate Coconut Keto Smoothie	Creamy Basil Baked Sausage	Keto Sausage Balls	Baked Rib Eye Steak with Grilled Vegetables

Thank You

To everyone who has picked up The Muscle Ladder Cookbook Inspired by Jeff Nippard Teachings, thank you. This book is more than just a collection of recipes—it's a guide, a companion, and a testament to the power of blending science with practicality in the pursuit of fitness excellence.

Your decision to invest in this cookbook shows your commitment to not just building a stronger body but also embracing the importance of proper nutrition as the cornerstone of your fitness journey. Whether you're a seasoned lifter, a weekend warrior, or just starting to explore the world of health and fitness, this book was created with you in mind. Every recipe, every tip, and every word was crafted to make your goals feel achievable, your progress tangible, and your meals enjoyable.

I want to express my deepest gratitude to Jeff Nippard for inspiring the principles and philosophies that shape this book. His dedication to evidence-based fitness has been a game-changer for so many, myself included. It's my hope that this cookbook honors his teachings and serves as a valuable resource for all who use it.

To you, the reader, thank you for trusting this book to be part of your fitness journey. It's your drive, discipline, and passion that make this work meaningful. Remember, progress isn't about perfection—it's about showing up, making small but consistent improvements, and staying committed to the process. Each meal you prepare and enjoy from this book is a step forward.

As you climb your own "muscle ladder," celebrate the wins, learn from the setbacks, and never forget why you started. Fitness is a lifelong journey, and this book is here to make that journey as effective, sustainable, and enjoyable as possible.

Here's to fueling your progress, one delicious recipe at a time. Stay strong, stay consistent, and keep striving for greatness.

Thank you for letting The Muscle Ladder Cookbook be part of your story.

With gratitude,

Michelle C. Huff

Author of The Muscle Ladder Cookbook

Made in United States
Orlando, FL
21 December 2024

56364290R10050